D1032152

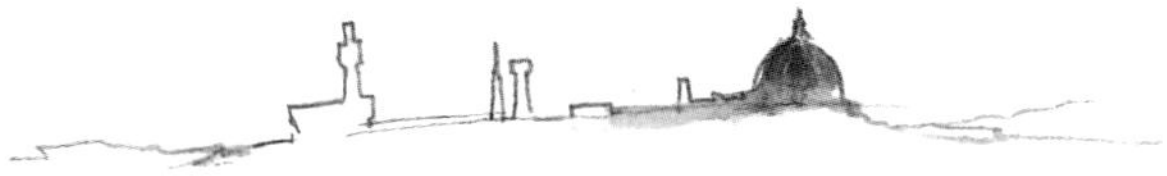

Andrea Ponsi

FLORENCE   *A Map of Perceptions*

305214049
R

University of Virginia Press
© 2010 by the Rector and Visitors of the University of Virginia
All rights reserved
Printed in China on acid-free paper

First published 2010

9 8 7 6 5 4 3 2 1

LIBRARY OF CONGRESS CATALOGING-IN-PUBLICATION DATA
Ponsi, Andrea.
   Florence : a map of perceptions / Andrea Ponsi.
       p.   cm.
   ISBN 978-0-8139-2873-9 (cloth : alk. paper)
   1. Florence (Italy)—Description and travel. 2. Florence
(Italy)—In art. I. Title.
   DG734.23.P67 2010
   914.5'5110493—dc22   2009012955

Enter | Enter the circle of walls through Porta Romana.

Follow along the road and enter the other side of the city, across the Ponte Vecchio.

Move under the arches of Vasari's corridor and enter the courtyard of the Uffizi.

From the Uffizi, enter into Piazza della Signoria.

Follow Via Calzaiuoli and enter the piazza of the Duomo.

There, cross the last door, the Door of Paradise, and enter the Baptistry.

And recognize, in the water of the primary fountain, the center and origin of the city.

Like a series of Chinese boxes, the city is made of rooms within rooms, joined by doors which are real or symbolic.

Walls | Walking along a street in the center of town, I raise an arm to graze the wall at my side, sensing through my fingertips the warm friction of the porous stone. I reach a copper downspout. My hand bumps over it, resting on the grainy stucco surface. I am interrupted by a cool door frame. Just a brief contact with its grooves, and I hop to the jamb on the other side, lightly brushing the wooden door as I do so. The wall I approach wears an iron hoop like an earring. This ring once held the reins of horses. I give in to the temptation to lift and then drop it, just to hear the metallic sound. I am passing by blocks carved in high relief; the palace is an important one and these cushions of stone deserve a caress. I near another doorway and lift my hand to the brass plaque, with its doorbells, cool to the touch. The portal is open and I leap across it in a two-meter flight. On the other side the stone is warmer, still in the sun. A bit uneven, it is flaking: winter frost and pietra serena don't coexist well. Only acrylic resins can stop the scaling. I restrain my touch, pressing lightly. There is a brief groove, and once again smooth stucco. I contribute to the patina with the dirt of my fingertip. By the end of the block of houses, the acute angle of the last corner is within sight. Like every good edge it has been treated like an ornament. An engaged column with a diameter of just a few centimeters rises up to the top of the palace. A final caress, and I lower my arm to join the cadence of my stride.

The Labyrinth | I live in a labyrinth city. I know only certain routes. The familiar ones are few in comparison to the many alien byways. From narrow shadowed streets, I see other alleys branching out to mysterious destinations. Only rarely do I enter them: searching for another street, a certain store, the house of a friend.

I have lived in Florence for many years, but still don't know it. I walk distracted, with my eyes roving the shop fronts, or fixed upon the gray stones underfoot. I look up at the gutters, their oblique edges outlining the jagged figure of sky, the closed windows and the barred doors; the secret palaces and inaccessible steeples. Yet I course through the city's veins, touching its muscles and, at times, penetrating its organs. As when, for example, I enter the City Hall in the Palazzo Vecchio.

First the courtyard, then up the wide staircase, and finally into the grand hall: the biggest room I have ever seen. The biggest one that still seems like a room, anyway. I am standing in the city's heart, feeling small and insignificant.

I crane my neck toward the ceiling. Above, every panel is an enormous oil canvas teeming with humans and horses, twisted into scenes of ancient battles. It is rare to see paintings parallel to the pavement; but it is rarer still to find oneself in such a paradoxical room. It is a piazza inside a building. A covered piazza which certain people, mostly city functionaries, cross diagonally. Their dry footsteps are loudly amplified in the space. The people who cross this room produce illusionary grand echoes because the enormous space makes everything seem enormous. And yet, the space simultaneously renders all things minute. Tiny the thousands of little tiles; tiny each painted face among the multitudes; tiny the gilded volutes of the Baroque frames.

Searching for a possible reference of scale I raise an open palm to span the entire space. When I draw my hand toward my eyes, the space shrinks further. I see the palm's network of lines only centimeters away, as it walls off the room. Between the fingers, a few cracks of light still penetrate. I touch my forehead, pressing the palm against my eyes. Now I see nothing. Only darkness, neither enormous nor small. Just obscurity, complete.

Order and the City | The medieval city is a tactile space; a compressed body made up of other compressed bodies. Collected within the narrow confines of the encircling city walls, it is an organic structure of sinuous routes, deep streets, and adjacent towers. Only with the piazzas, open to the sky if secular, covered when inside churches and the cathedral, does this body open up to greet the community.

During the Renaissance another idea was appended to the clear hierarchy between urban fabric and the open space of the piazza: that of the directional cut, of the measured widening, regular and geometric. Via dei Servi, the Hospital of the Innocents, the dome of the cathedral, all create a superimposed system of

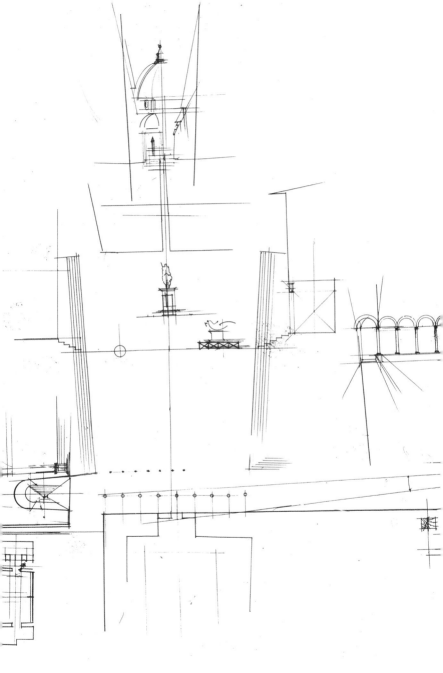

orientation that transcends the centripetal order of the medieval city, enlarging the urban experience toward the countryside and the whole region.

With Mannerism and the Baroque, the city proceeded in this dynamic settlement pattern and her image was enriched by a helicoidal and spiraling vision. But for Florence, those were not the years of highest splendor, and the spiral was kept tight.

There is no true neoclassical Florence, but there is an eclectic Florence based on nineteenth-century classicism. It was then that the medieval spatiality, tactile and narrow, was definitively negated, opened, eviscerated like an animal. Thus the space of the present Piazza della Repubblica, the boulevards where there had been city walls, the huge piazzas at the new perimeter of the city, all clearly exhibit the result of this decisive cleaning followed by a vigorous urban centrifuge. It was nonetheless an operation conducted with a certain style, still based on a sane, academic sense of proportions. From the potential Baroque spiral order one passed to a new model: a sort of dynamic square expanding, undulating from the center of the city outward to the perimeter.

Defining the spatial analogy that Florence acquired in this last century is a difficult task. References to Euclidean geometry are unhelpful. One speaks instead of the linear city, the city of tentacles, of expansion "like an oil drop." Above all, of a city that destroys itself through enlargement. The city loses its ordering structure and rarefies itself without creating new poles of aggregation, as well as losing its own center. Space, undefined by geometry, becomes subservient to traffic, speculation, abstract zonification. It seems an impossible task to control, direct, and concretely impose form. However, before entering into the vortex of discussions, proposals, and projects, it seems that there is, at least metaphorically, one thing to do: stop. Stop the construction of every new building and the destruction of every old edifice. Stop the proliferation of offices and shops; the occupation of the piazzas; the intrusion into every last remnant of countryside. Block the traffic, stay in the house, stop walking. We are halted, like statues, arms suspended, bodies leaning, eyes wide. And then, as if petrified, we wait. Only when we have calmed our breathing, experienced the absolute silence, rediscovered the rhythm of wisdom, only then can we perhaps begin to investigate the city's true nature. And what we would like it to be, and how it could be built.

Two Cities | Florence is not silent. At least not in the streets, in the loggias, in the markets, in the piazzas. Florence is rambunctious, busy, noisy. Silence

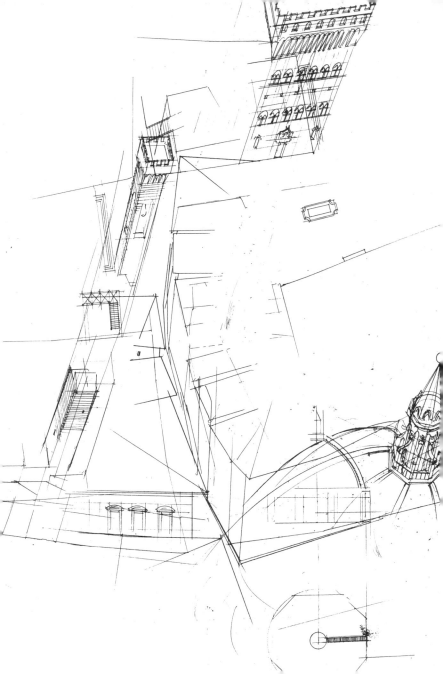

in Florence exists, but is secret. It is hidden behind the gates, at the end of the tunnels of vestibules which open onto the courtyards and gardens. There the silence dominates, rarefied between the little paths of rubble, in the humidity of the grottoes, between the boxwood and the fountains. But still deeper and more secret is the silence of the cloisters in the convents. They are innumerable within the city, yet somehow removed from it. Here the quiet is everywhere: in the rhythm of the vaults, in the light which bathes the columns, in the simple, squared profile of the space against the sky.

Florence is a divided city, half harmonious and half chaotic; half a place of action, half of reflection. Side by side, divided by a hallway or a wall on the street, the two worlds live together symbiotically, nurturing each other with the contrast they create.

The Flight | Sometimes I fly above the city. From high up I see the forms of the bell towers, the pure octagons of the domes, the lightning rods with rampant bronze lions, so close I could touch them.

When I fly, I see the pigeons asleep under the roof tiles. I follow the movement of the heads of the tourists who have climbed the towers. The river reflects the clouds and the cars become colored dominoes. I skim the TV antennas, then regain altitude, feeling a touch of vertigo, flying extremely high. I hardly notice the lines of cypresses, the isolated villas, the rustic farmhouses, while the river has become a luminous rivulet of sun.

Via Laura | I rediscover Via Laura anew, every time I climb the stairs of my basement studio. At midpoint, I can see, through the glass door, the glimmer of the ocher wall across the street. It runs almost the entire length of the street and is probably the longest unbroken surface in the city. A few months ago, restoration of the Archeological Museum, which faces Via Laura, was completed. The wall briefly remained perfect and pristine; a huge ocher surface, uniform, almost too homogenous. The usual graffiti soon reappeared. So now the lower part, along its entire length, is an arabesque of proclamations, invective, exhortations, and curses. Two factions of graffiti fighters wage war on this perpendicular battleground. They fire scribbled fusillades in their chosen colors of red and black. The red represents the Left—"Radical Revolutionaries"—and the black identifies the Right— "The Fronte," the fascists. And even if the messages are a bit ambiguous, the abstract designs are pleasant enough. I no longer read the messages, however. I just notice the patterns. The highest part of the wall, beyond the comfortable reach of a wielded can of spray paint, remains untouched. And this illustrates how the scale of the human body determines our perceptions and comprehension of the city.

Anyway, I am still standing in my doorway, looking at the latest graffiti skirmish. And only now do I notice the groups of passing students, laughing and shoving, on their way to the nearby Faculty of Political Science. No one comes here any longer by bus or on foot. They arrive on mopeds or Vespas, or they ride those new types of motorbikes that are like animal mutations. A line of parked cars is a distant memory in Via Laura. Now there is only one continuous line of two-wheelers positioned like a spine. Two machines per meter equals two hundred for every hundred meters, on a street two hundred meters long equals four hundred mopeds. Four hundred license plates, four hundred headlights, seats, chains, locks. One has an urge to knock one over and start them falling like dominoes.

In any case, Via Laura remains one of the streets with a distinguishing identity. Two flying passages bridge the street where Via Laura meets Via della Pergola. These arches become skyborne portals in the middle of the street, making it seem more intimate. They join blocks of houses and wings of former convents, suggesting an alternative, autonomous city built above the street. In reality, the whole neighborhood is made of connected old convents.

There are other streets like Via Laura, such as Via della Colonna and Via Capponi, crossed by arches. But these arches are nothing other than visible fragments of a suspended labyrinth made of corridors, galleries, tunnels, and secret passages.

I close the door behind me, turn right, and walk along the center of the road. The paving stones are broad and massive, cut into uneven shapes, and fitted together like a puzzle. I do not try to avoid the cracks, as children often do. A few steps and I am at the end of the street. I turn left and it vanishes. Peering into the shadows ahead, already I can make out the play of the perfectly proportioned loggias and sculptures of Piazza Santissima Annunziata.

From the Terrace | Each time I go up on the roof terrace the scene is replayed: a fan shape of architecture emerges with the evenness of isolated Platonic solids. Few major cities have Florence's visual expression of powerful monuments, although this is, on a lesser scale, a general characteristic of the medieval city, especially in central Italy. In these towns and cities, the cathedral, the city hall, the basilica's steeples, and various towers rise above the homogeneous horizon of houses. The cityscape resembles a chessboard: one can see the objects from various viewpoints, creating new, layered

vistas. When such a chessboard is enlarged to the scale of the city, and one lives in it, with its actual horizon, weather conditions, and variations of light, it is one of the most spectacular visions that architecture can offer.

From the terrace of my house the cathedral's dome and the tower of the Palazzo Vecchio become equivalent in size and hierarchy. They are in fact the same distance from here and create a dialogue among equals. The center of the vacant space between them is marked by the pair formed by the steeple of the Badia and the tower of the Bargello.

By contrast, from the terrace of my friend L——, near Palazzo Pitti, the relation between the monuments is completely different. There, the grandiose façade of the Pitti Palace prevails, and then, in descending order of size, the tower of the Palazzo Vecchio and, just beside it, yet much farther away, the dome of the cathedral. One can see, however, the highest parts of the colored façade of Santa Maria Novella and Santa Croce.

Yet again, in Via Ricasoli, from the terrace of M——, the imposing presence of the dome distorts all proportional balance. Seen from so near, it is a mountain of light which annuls the power of all the other architecture. Nevertheless, from that spot unforeseen configurations form, even if they are still composed of Arnolfo's Tower, the mass of the churches, the Bargello and the Badia, the Forte di Belvedere. They are the familiar characters reordered into fresh visions.

Via della Ninna | One of the characteristics of Florence's urban pattern is the recurring presence of an accidental geometry based on acute angles, deriving from the irregular street network. This singularity becomes evident while one is looking upward at the intersection of streets. The strong corners of the gutters and the corresponding voids of the streets meet at their diagonal axis. This "wedge" effect is also evident at ground level in those radial crossings where five or six streets come together, or in the angled edges of almost every piazza. This irregularity enters the interiors of houses and palaces, and repeats itself throughout. And the wedge-shaped space of many rooms reverberates through the constant memory of the city's form. It is as if the regular grid of Roman Florence had suffered a near-irreversible cultural and geometric earthquake from which it was impossible to recover. Even the rude eighteenth-century intervention, intended to re-create that order by destroying and reconstructing the Old Market neighborhood, could not restore the lost spirit of the original grid. And so the image of the

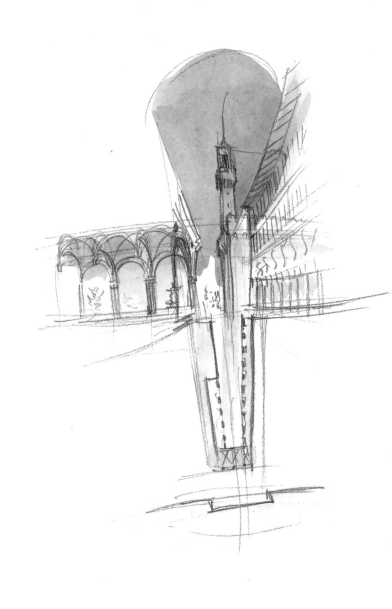

geometrically irregular urban layout of Florence has remained almost unaltered.

With its varied levels of complexity, the intersection of the Uffizi Piazzale, Via della Ninna, and Piazza della Signoria illustrates this peculiar condition. At this point the edges of the three volumes of the Loggia dei Lanzi, the Palazzo Vecchio, and the Uffizi museum converge at irregular angles. The axis of the Piazzale degli Uffizi is slightly divergent with respect to Palazzo Vecchio, so the view of the building is eccentric and oblique. In turn, the palace itself is a structure which is based on a strongly asymmetrical condition. In fact, the tower is cantilevered and asymmetric to the façade. Coherent with this geometry, the natural and best viewpoint of the palace is the diagonal one from the outside edge, a view actually accentuated by the presence of the Neptune fountain. The eccentricity of the tower emphasizes the imbalance, creating in turn a new dynamic equilibrium.

The secret of the intersection with Via della Ninna, besides this irregular geometry, is the parallel tension that is created among solids and voids. At street level, one sees on one side the solid prism of Palazzo Vecchio. The huge *pietra forte* stones are rough cut and naturalistic, creating the illusion of fortresslike rock walls. For contrast, on the opposite side, the hollowed-out solid of the Loggia dei Lanzi opens but doesn't lose the sense of volume on the corner thanks to the presence of its grand composite pier. This rises powerfully, like an ancient tree that divides into the arcuated members of the ribs. These great arches give the compressed space of the intersection a necessary release and simultaneously make the loggia seem like a covered continuation of Via della Ninna. On the Uffizi side, the edge is defined at the street level by a pier which allows a fluid spatial movement around it. At the upper floors of the building the space closes up again, transforming from loggia into palace, while the building's surface becomes a vibrant game of projections of pilasters, plaques, and cornices. Here, everything revolves around the chromatic contrast between the white of the stucco and the gray of the *pietra serena*.

The fourth and final corner is absent and thus represents the true invention of the place. Instead of a corner there is the opening to Piazza della Signoria. The intersection therefore becomes the doorway, the point of maximum compression previous to the release into the huge open space. Yet before we can gaze toward the piazza with its statues, and above the roofs, the emerging mass of Orsanmichele, we are drawn, as if by a dynamic force, toward the grand vaults of the Loggia

dei Lanzi and the long perspective of the Uffizi. Then, once again, toward Via della Ninna, which recedes into the dense fabric of the city. It is hard to overpower the forceful attraction that holds us in the center of that tight intersection of streets. It is not easy to pull ourselves away from that point where all the magnetic forces of the city seem to converge.

Piazza Santo Spirito | Like an elongated trapeze inclined along its own axis of symmetry, Piazza Santo Spirito finds its unmistakable identity in the grand façade of the church: a suspended curtain, white as a bedsheet.

The edges of the piazza are defined by a wall of houses homogeneous of form, rhythm, and scale. Houses lived in, furthermore, by people from the neighborhood, and not yet turned into offices. There is also, as expected, the patriarchal palazzo with the top-floor loggia, spacious and cool in the summer. Miraculously, the Bandini sisters' *pensione* still occupies this privileged site.

Off the beaten path, it is the only major piazza ringed by trees. Each morning it becomes a market-place; in the afternoon, a sleepy retreat. At night the place draws a various crowd, straitlaced and transgressive, from all over the city.

Piazza Santa Croce | While sitting on a stone bench in Piazza Santa Croce, I think back to the past and all the times I have sat on this same bench. As a small child, I used to sit here when my parents brought me to Florence to visit some distant relative. In the middle of the piazza the statue of Dante rose from the mass of parked cars. Piazza della Signoria, too, had become clogged with tourist buses. And car owners, with a bit of luck, could even park in front of the Duomo.

Then I see myself in the early seventies, dressed in blue jeans and a T-shirt. I'm not so much seated as draped over this stone bench—a suntanned student watching his friends slice the piazza in diagonals with a frisbee. This was possible because Dante had been banished to the damp ground behind the church, where he lay supine. Later, by popular demand, he was cleaned and restored to his pedestal, but moved to a new site right beside the church. I remember the small crowd watching the crane lift him through the air, where he hung suspended, resembling an unskilled tightrope walker, or a vulnerable invalid being helped to a seat. In the new location he leveled his severe stare directly at his former post. In those days, cars could still park at the sides of the piazza, in front of the old stores, the electrician's workshop, the first gold shops for tourists.

For a long time I didn't go to Piazza Santa Croce. Then toward the end of the eighties when I returned to live in Florence, I discovered again that this bench was an excellent spot, especially on Sunday mornings in winter, to catch the sun, to lay open my newspaper, to reflect on the human paradox of the tourist who takes photographs without looking, to watch new gold shops and stands with rows of plastic Davids sprouting up. I looked for signs of continuity. An old man leaning on his cane, kids playing soccer, students lounging around on the benches, the announcement of a good exhibition at the Pananti Gallery, by then squeezed between a Salvador Dalí museum and a new money-changing office.

Now I often come here to read, watch, listen, and think, and I realize that everything has changed and yet everything is unchanged. The skin on my hands has changed. My hair has been cut, grown, cut, grown, dozens of times; also changed are the clothes I wear, my thoughts, my dreams. The very blood coursing through my veins has altered on its circulatory journey. Cells in my bones are transformed every second.

So everything in the piazza is changed: The pigeons, many generations removed from those that landed near me years ago. The marble of the church, milled, polished, injected with resins. On the ground, the stones have been corroded by water or worn into tiny pieces, some of which might travel to Japan, wedged in the soles of a tourist's shoes. On the roofs, new tiles have replaced broken ones. Fresh paint coats the shutters. And every day, the leaves of that ivy plant on the wall of that same terrace grow and die.

Yet, amid this continuous variation, I am still myself, seated here on this same stone bench, in this same piazza which, though different, remains my old piazza, still herself.

Santissima Annunziata | As in a game I see a geometry of imaginary lines interwoven upon the piazza. They are made by the scooter which, oblivious to the regulations, cuts through it diagonally. By the man with the hat who walks only in the company of his shadow. By the aerodynamic pigeon. By the slow, single, white cloud. By the heavy-lidded gazes of the students sitting on the steps.

There is no actual grid here, but I envisage a chessboard implied by the rhythm of the porticoes, the vertical rectangles, and the columns at their sides. The people become the pawns, the fountains the bishops, and Prince Ferdinand on his horse of course is the king.

The Bargello and the Badia | If we were to compare the monuments of the skyline of Florence to a family, wherein (setting aside building chronology) the figure of the father would be embodied by Palazzo Vecchio and its tower, and that of the mother by Santa Maria del Fiore and her dome, we would find the children of this well-suited couple in the tower of the Bargello and the steeple of the Badia.

Close to each other in the city center, and of similar height, they stand equally near their parents.

The civic Bargello, with its square tower ornamented by the vertical appendages of crenellations and shields, with its cubic and regular body, mirrors the Palazzo Vecchio in all aspects.

The Badia, her steeple with lacelike ornament, pointed like Brunelleschi's lantern and faceted like the archetypal octagon turning centrifugally to the whole community, is the spiritual reverberation of the massive octagon of the cathedral's cupola.

Brother and sister then, rendered siblings even by the color and consistency of their skin of stone. That of the Bargello is marked by freckles of red bricks. That of the Badia waits to be clad in appropriate garments. Indeed, in that first primitive and corporeal vision of Florence, the fresco of the Loggia del Bigallo, she is represented

dressed up in the multicolored marble so similar to that
of her mother cathedral.

The Duomo | I have entered the Duomo and crossed
the length of the central nave, and now I am seated on
a bench in front of the altar in the right apse, where I
can examine the stained glass. Traced with lines of lead,
the figures of the saints are all framed within images of
little rooms which are narrow microspaces, almost like
second suits of architecture. Underneath every glass
window are frescoes, and even here the painted figures
are framed by rooms of architecture. Under the central
fresco stands the altar with a miniature model of a
Gothic tabernacle resting on it. Inside is the figure of a
saint.

Now I study the piers, the building's real architecture. Attached to the major ones, like bas-reliefs, are
various aedicules: little classical temples projecting from
the brackets. In the temples between small columns,
protected by the pediment, stand the statues of human
figures. Each niche, every arched bay, every aedicule in
turn contains a statue, and each statue is enclosed and
protected by its own architecture.

I widen my gaze to embrace the entire space of
the apse. It frames no central figure. Rather, in this
case the figure is universal and fickle, divided into

various components: it is composed of all those people who, like me, are sitting here resting and praying and thinking. The apse is our frame. But in its turn, like the other two apses, it is enclosed and protected by the central dome. The dome doesn't surmount a specific figure. The object of its protection is in fact the entire urban community. Indeed, high on the horizon of the city, the dome transcends its specific confines and becomes the vault that frames and protects the entire region.

Waves | If the roofs of Florence were waves, the tiles would be the spray of foam, the pigeons seagulls, the streets deep whirlpools. The TV antennas would be twigs that break the surface, the terraces drifting rafts, churches and basilicas the hulls of boats. The hills would be islands, the towers lighthouses, the crenellations reefs.

Via dei Servi | Walking along Via dei Servi, I follow the rhythm of the windows and cornice lines of the roofs that razor into the sky. At the end of the street is the greenish wall of the cathedral, yellower at its base, perhaps from sunset's transitory light. Or perhaps, more prosaically, because it hasn't been cleaned for a while. My eye ascends the mountain of marble, disentangling me from the spirals of stone, leaded windows, and iron rods. Then I start up the curved rise of the dome, a shell of terra-cotta scales, slippery like the skin of a giant fish. All the forces consolidate at the summit. The ribs coalesce in a lacework of marble, forming the lantern temple, white and perfect.

The River | The river cleaves the city in two. It's a fickle river, defined less by water than by its banks of stone and the palaces which line it, forming long ornate walls. In the winter the Arno takes shape; it swells, often angrily. It collects the water from half of Tuscany, and all that water rushes past its narrowest point as if through a funnel. That point coincides with the very center of the city. There it flows under the three low arches of the Ponte Vecchio, then widens again to continue toward the plain and, finally, the sea.

By July it becomes a gutter of yellowish slime that crawls through reeds, bushes, and banks of mud so vast that they are used as parking lots. Whoever goes down there discovers a different world, more silent and rural. One can walk along these natural embankments and rest upon the grass near the bridges.

Few bridges cross the river, and each that does is different from the others. The Ponte Vecchio is a continuation of the urban fabric, an umbilical cord

made of houses between two banks of buildings. It is bridge, piazza, loggia, and street all in one; with its tower, shops, and houses, it is a true city in miniature. From the opening at its center, the hills flow out on one side, the sun sets on the other. When I sit on the stone railing I feel as if I am on the needle arm of a balancing scale, on the perfect point of equilibrium between the two parts of the city. From here, looking west, one sees the next bridge, the most elegant of all, Santa Trinita. Three wide arches soar over the water as in a dance. Their curves are so harmonious that the eye would never tire of looking at them. Some have said it is the most beautiful bridge in the world. Certainly it is the most beautiful that I have ever seen.

Via delle Pinzochere | Via delle Pinzochere is a short and narrow street of twenty houses and palaces. My house sits at its center. In one direction, from my third-floor window, I can see the loggia of Santa Croce at the street's end. In the other direction, the street stops at the door of Michelangelo's house. Just beyond arm's reach I see the facing windows of the opposite house. The street is grayish, dulled by the stone pavement and the dark stucco of the unrestored façades damaged by the 1966 flood. The one noble palace has an entry door surmounted by radial ashlar stones, and three floors of large Renaissance windows. It's skirted by a long bench of stone. My son likes to walk on it, and I often sit there, waiting for someone to exit my house. Sidewalks are minimal. Most people walk in the street unless a passing car forces them up against the buildings. Via delle Pinzochere is a quiet street. But it's not unusual to see someone seated in a doorway, preparing his fix.

The Unfinished Façades | San Lorenzo, the Cestello, and the Carmine all have façades that were never finished. Because of this, the piazzas in front of them also remain unfinished. If at that time the builders had not, out of an exalted sense of "civility," finished the façades of the Duomo and of Santa Croce, then Florence would truly have been the "city of the unfinished." But at the end of the nineteenth century, there was a great need for certainty. Now, more certain of our uncertainties, we no longer feel the need to finish things. Our own certainty is merely that of the infinite, and since that is by definition the unfinished, the uncompleted façade is in reality for us "infinite." From this issues our true security: the security of our doubt. How could we do without it? And why should we cover up these mirrors? After all, where else would we ever find as clear a picture of our inconsistency?

The Observatory of Arcetri | At the end of the straight avenue rising to Poggio Imperiale, on the left, beyond a field of olive trees and among the cypresses, appear the domes of the observatory of Arcetri. Like planets in a terrestrial sky, a minor sphere orbits beside a larger white one. Further beyond protrudes a fragment of the inclined parabolic disk.

Arcetri is a celestial monastery which at night, when the telescopes are fixed upon the stars, becomes the supreme roof, the highest terrace in the city. From up there the lights of an inattentive world are only a distant reverberation.

On the Bicycle | Given the natural and unappreciated predisposition of the historic center of Florence to bicycle riding, here is a list of the most common types of road conditions. I've judged them relative to their adaptability to two-wheeled travel:

Irregular slabs of gray stone: These retain the memory of the antique Roman *opus incertum* and are often uneven, causing jolting from the gentle to the severe. In any case, they should never be substituted with alternative paving, but only repaired, replacing the damaged pieces. It is the type of paving most in sympathy with the character of Florence: durable and philologically correct, and thus undoubtedly the best.

Regular cut stones: In parallel lines, almost always installed in the pattern of a fish spine. They are stippled to minimize slipperiness in wet weather. In the past hand-chiseled, they are now incised with a pneumatic drill. These stones create a sufficiently smooth condition, especially when formed by blocks that have been cut recently. Passing over them, the wheels constantly vibrate, producing a pleasant ringing sound.

Sanpietrini (cobblestones): Not a local stone, which is obvious from its name. They were used to repave many nineteenth-century streets in the historic center ("restored to new life"). For bicycles, they provide a surface which is passable if well maintained, painful when poorly maintained, and dangerous if two or more adjacent stones are missing. You can get your tire stuck in the small cracks and be thrown into the street. And until twenty years ago, the *sanpietrini*-paved streets still bore evidence of the tram tracks, perilous for bicyclists. These crevices seemed custom-made to the width of bicycle tires, and the unbalanced rider, trying to regain equilibrium, inevitably took a spill. Anyway, the problem no longer exists. The idea of reinstating the tram was unwisely abandoned, and the old tracks were covered with new layers of asphalt.

Asphalt: The best surface for a fast and smooth ride, with minimal wear on the tires. It makes a continuous rustling sound, a kind of hum that lets you hear the rolling of the wheel on the hub, or the links of the gear chain. In any case, it's an anonymous experience. Asphalt is the most harmful surface for the city's memory and perception of its beauty. Considered an appropriate material for a poured fill, it was used for the resurfacing of most sidewalks and streets in the sixties and seventies. Now it is obvious that it has ruined beautiful streets: Via Cavour, Via Romana, Via della Vigna Nuova, and dozens of others.

Concrete: A paving substance that, even though limited to just two or three streets in the city center, still assumes a very high symbolic value. Cycling is totally irrelevant relative to the outrage that Florence suffered during the thirties when whole sections of the historical district of Santa Croce were destroyed in the name of "urban reclamation." The new streets were made, in a style consistent with the era, with concrete slabs resembling the German motorways of Hitler. Anyway, it makes a very hard street surface, very costly to replace with an alternative. It is, however, necessary to do so.

Fiesole | When seen from Florence, the hill of Fiesole appears a sinuous hollow between two promontories. As one approaches from the city, the hill displays the magnificence of an Olympic cliff, adorned with

cypresses, pines, and villas. But one perceives something
arid in this environment—like the slopes which sur-
round a Greek acropolis. Here, the Etruscan Fiesole
rediscovers and consolidates its Greek memory, even
though the Roman theater and baths dominate the hill's
opposite slope.

Tuscany, from the Center | I have stopped on the
Ponte Vecchio at sunset and am standing in the spot
in the middle of the bridge where the wall of shops is
interrupted for a brief space and the view opens onto
the river to the west. Far away, beyond the clouds tinged
with red, one can discern the outline of the Apuan
Alps. Today, it is a western breeze that combs waves
into the Arno and blows the surface of the water back
upstream: down there beyond the mountains, a stiff
wind will batter the coast for three days. On the coast,
at Viareggio, at Forte dei Marmi, the sun is setting, as it
is here now.

   I lean over the stone railing. The rumpled surface of
the river's green water reflects the violet clouds above
it. I turn and crane over the opposite side of the bridge,
where to the east a dark grayish-maroon sky backs
the rows of cypresses climbing the hills toward San
Miniato. Beyond that there is the blue profile of the hills

encircling the city, then the higher mountains of the
Apennines, then Pratomagno, Arezzo, the Casentino
valley.

I stand in the center of the bridge, of the city, of the
course of the river, of its valley between the mountains
and the sea; I am in the center of Tuscany. The point
I describe is a point suspended over the water, at the
summit of an arch made of stone, at the moment when
day turns to night: a point in the center of time.

Piazza della Signoria | Now it is only a life-sized
copy, a man along with twenty or thirty other men
and women fixed forever in marble and bronze. In the
sixteenth century, when it was placed in the Piazza
della Signoria, the David, the original one, was the only
human being next to the sculpted lions on the Loggia
dei Lanzi. Now he is one among many giants, such as
the somewhat flaccid Neptune, such as Hercules and
Cacus, such as the groups engaged in bodily combat and
arranged at measured distances from each other. White
bodies like the skin of the captured Sabine woman or
the bodies, dusty with smog, of warriors who fought in
the real dust. Green bodies of bronze like those of the
lascivious nymphs on the fountain of Neptune or the
Sovereign Prince on his enormous horse.

Lower down, on the pavement of the square, hundreds of bodies are in motion, walking, crouching to the ground to study tourist maps, or crowding around a guide who points and explains, equipped with a loudspeaker. Bodies dressed in blue jeans, T-shirts, multicolored bags, belts, sweaters. Here are some groups of Japanese tourists, protected from the sun by colorful umbrellas. Everything is moving, waving, shimmering: blond, red, brown, gray, black hair; straw hats, baseball caps, golf visors; even the birds dart in fits and starts, pecking at the ground or taking flight in flocks. Half of the square, the lower half, is alive—dynamic, messy, tacky; the other half, the upper one, dominates—austere, immortal, petrified in gestures frozen in time.

The Chapel of the Magi (Palazzo Medici Riccardi) | In the rarest of circumstances a structure may house a vision in which man and landscape mirror each other in an atmosphere of dreamy symbiosis. In the Chapel of the Magi, every wall is painted with this harmony. A procession of people dressed in fabrics decorated with garland patterns snakes along among tame animals, white rocks, slender trunks of elegant cypress trees. The birds look like clouds and the clouds like birds; the clumps of grass are as sinuous as the blond curls of the pages. A jaguar sits beside a man on horseback; the serene hawk eats his meal just as nature decrees. Color suffuses everything, and the procession's supernatural progress across the landscape can be felt as physically as a light wind. Everything is at once mobile and marvelously poised within the scene. There are no empty corners. The castle in the background is surrounded by beech woods, the manicured olive trees punctuate the hillsides, the unpaved roads descend to the valley bottom like slow streams. Four walls of complete harmony, four horizons of happy life.

Against the back wall, at a slight distance in the little niche, an altarpiece painted on wood reminds us of the real protagonists of this place of worship and the final goal of the procession: the humble stable of the Holy Family.

The Loggia del Mercato Nuovo | They are taking down the wheeled stands that all day long have filled the noisy and unruly marketplace under the roof of the Loggia del Porcellino, or the Mercato Nuovo, which is its real name. It is easier now to see the ceiling: a sky of "sail" vaults hanging above a forest of *pietra serena* trees. Little by little, amid the clanking of folded metal frames, the screech of carts, the thunk of boards slamming shut, the voices and shouts of the men pulling this caravan away to a nearby garage, the

broad polished floor of the large loggia reappears. The covered square is visible again, the pigeons once more hop around in search of crumbs or pieces of ice-cream cones. The loggia-palace-square-forest-sky traversed by twelve voluminous clouds can finally breathe again—free, silent, shining; ready to host the night and the few passersby who give it an admiring glance as they walk past.

The Roman Amphitheater | The Roman Amphitheater reveals, as a reminder of what it once was, only its vertical oval surface facing onto deep streets. This elliptical footprint, now covered with houses, roofs, and terraces, is easily visible in its entirety only if you look at a map of the city. Over time, the void of the arena has been filled in and the perfect oval has been hewn into three parts by the knives of streets. The curve remains, continuous, slightly faceted due to the straight façade of each individual house, creating an event different from any other in the city. Inside the houses, arranged like the spokes of a wheel, can still be seen the stone or *opus incertum* walls, the vaults made of long, thin bricks, the cement of long ago. And maybe also, embedded in the ruins, pieces of skin, fragments of clothes, the footprints and the shouts of ancient sports fans.

Another Duomo | Once upon a time, the Duomo was inhabited by statues of martyrs, saints, and prophets. These sculptures occupied every recess of the ancient façade; every niche, exedra, and pointed arch of the large portals. Inside the Duomo, other men, women, and animals made up the sculpted population of this concave universe. Today those faces, bodies, full tunics of marble, horses, birds, and lions have been moved into a museum created for this purpose just a few steps away, and replaced by copies. The Museo dell'Opera del Duomo consists of a series of rooms in which an artificial and unreal condition has been re-created as a memory of the house that once was. Halogen lights, concrete pedestals, wooden display boards are the furnishings of the new rooms in this hotel for evicted tenants. Or rather, refugees from the polluted atmosphere, the vandals, or simply the neglect that would have awaited them. Now the observer, the tourist, can get close to the statues and admire every detail, and this is a conquest. Before, they could only be seen from far away, inserted into some niche suspended dozens of meters high. Now, they can be touched. Our marvel is great at seeing the skill of the chiseling, the elegant handling of the veils, the waves of hair designed in marble. Now everything is right at hand, like an animal behind bars in an exquisitely designed zoo.

Postscriptum on the Museo dell'Opera del Duomo | One room of the museum is devoted to the stone plaques that have been moved here from their original location along the outer perimeter of Giotto's bell tower. Their new position gives us a new perspective. Not only can we get just a few inches away from them, but by sitting on the bench in the middle of the room and turning our heads, we can look at all forty-two of them at the same time, mounted on the four walls inside the room. The original view is inverted. The original convex arrangement on the outside of the bell tower, looking out, has become a concave arrangement looking in along the four walls of the room. Before, every plaque looked out onto the square. Now each plaque looks at the other plaques. The museum transforms reality; it overturns it, betrays it. And yet it offers a new version of reality, open to other sensations, new interpretations.

Piazza della Repubblica | Downtown Florence is like the torso of a human body. Following this analogy of urban anatomy, Piazza del Duomo corresponds to the heart, the center of the soul and spirit. Like a heart, its red dome pulsates with life.

The head is Piazza della Signoria: rational in the clear geometry of the Uffizi buildings; ambitious and powerful in the rocky mass of Palazzo Vecchio and its tower.

The belly is what is now Piazza della Repubblica: a place that feels only the stimulus of trade, impregnated with the smell of pastry shops, nineteenth-century cafés, the ice cream of today. A place that was a belly even before it was gutted in the late nineteenth century: the place devoted to meat, vegetables, and the "porch of the fishmongers," the Loggia del Pesce. The Old Market, which was greasy and dirty, vital with smells, was destroyed and "restored to new life," giving it a new menu, new tablecloth, crystal glassware, and a centerpiece of a monarch riding a horse. This king, not by his own fault, was later moved to the Parco delle Cascine. The square (or the table) is now empty in the center; one feels that it is lacking an object regal enough to reign there.

In Front of Palazzo Medici Riccardi | The palaces of the early Florentine Renaissance, like Palazzo Strozzi and Palazzo Medici Riccardi, are generally divided into three horizontal bands. The lowest one, which makes up the base, is composed of massive blocks hewn of *pietra forte,* jutting out from the surface of the façade. This layer presents itself as a thick curtain wall of stones, where only a few deep fissures covered with iron grates hint at some use for the space inside. It is the

most evident layer of the palace/fortress, an austere and impenetrable bastion of defense.

The middle band corresponds to the *piano nobile,* the state apartments. Here the rough surface of the base becomes more refined, emphasizing a geometry of thin lines of stones cut to resemble an elegant musical score etched into the wall. Above the large two-light windows, the score becomes a veritable fan, a perfect radial pattern that celebrates the shape of the arch.

On the top floor, corresponding to the third layer, even the etched lines disappear, and the wall becomes a smooth stone surface on which the delicate design of the windows divided by slender stone colonnettes stands out.

The palace terminates with a protruding cornice: a perfect rhythm of corbels carved with acanthus leaves, toothing, and dentilation echoing Greek and Roman times, the symbol of civilization, refinement, and classical measure.

The Renaissance palace's stratification in horizontal layers is analogous to the human condition. Rooted in the soil, overbearing in the fight for survival; balanced, peaceful, and harmonious in daily life and the family. Aesthetic, ideal, celestial in its highest aspirations: those which, like the decorated stone cornice, are closest to the heavens.

The Station | It is said that the Florence train station, seen from above, looks like a sheaf—the Fascist emblem. Maybe it does, but the reality is that this still represents an injection of modernity into the ancient center of the city. It is a big wall, similar to a modern Palazzo Pitti, a big covered square, like so many downtown. It is a cascade of glass that mirrors the older one, on the other side of the square, of the apse of Santa Maria Novella. It is a simple, clear sign, monumental but not rhetorical, sedate but not static, high on a pedestal but not dominating. It is an intelligent sign, authentic for its time, resistant to the tempests of fashion, functional in everyday life; a friendly sign, silent enough to be considered an accomplice, original enough that something may be learned from it.

The Green Riverbank | Ten meters down from where I am standing, unapproachable because no paths reach it, there is a little piece of earth on the bank of the Arno that disappears in winter under mud and water. A green meadow has blossomed here, with flowers just barely opening. Rats, nutrias, and snakes may be sleeping there now. The water is barely rippled, dark and deep like the night around me.

Trembling reflections of the street lamps and

windows appear on the water, and behind that a big
wall, the high bank that marks the line of the inhabited
world. Beyond that runs an illuminated strip of buildings. Some windows there are feeble mouths of light;
almost all are closed, mute as to whether or not there
is any life behind them. Inside the buildings many
people are asleep at this hour. What do they know
now of the colors of the world, of the stones, of the
asphalt, of the occasional streetlights? Nothing, and
nothing either of the little leaves shivering in the wind,
of the bush that grows on this untamed riverbank, this
meadow of pure nature. It too hides its life: rats, snakes,
worms, ants; digging, gliding, or sleeping next to the
river as it runs along.

Via Santo Spirito | 5 – Stop – Ice-cream shop –
"Give up" – 12 – National Institute of Statistics –
2nd floor – Driveway – Castorina Furniture Store –
CK86615 – CK784XN – Driveway – Restaurant –
Wednesday even side – midnight to 6 A.M. along the
entire street – FAAC automatic gate – Lanfredini Tower
13th–14th century – Beauty and well-being – 42 –
Number One – Stop – Pedestrian area – Ceni
Frescioni Lenti Bucci Strehlke – Notary Public –
Law Firm – DF974PL – 0-24 – A&L Carpets –
"Francesco Ferrucci was born in this house on 14 August

1489 and died bravely at Gavinana on 3 August 1530, and Florentine liberty fell with him" – Angela Caputi – Leave the passageway free – Darling I love you – except – Italy-Russia Cultural Association – European Federalist Movement – Nice 41 – electrical vehicles – Quadrifoglio operating machinery – Authorized access to Limited Traffic Zone – 6:00–9:30 A.M. 6:00–7:30 P.M. – residents' vehicles with sticker – authorization ord. – Via Santo Spirito.

A street is also what is written on it: graffiti, notices, names, signs, rhetorical plaques, house numbers. The life of a street is in the names of the people living there, in the bureaucratic restrictions, in the plates on the cars parked on it. It is the typographical present, the writing of the national language, the typeface of a hundred silent announcements. It is the imprint of the moment, of the permanent signs and of the temporary ones.

Piazza del Carmine | The 1966 flood reduced this square, like almost all the public squares in Florence, to a tragic pile of mud. Cars were floating belly-up like dead fish. The fury of the water had flayed them into carcasses. Forever? No! Instead, they have multiplied and, like the world's population, have increased in a spiraling progression. Now cars cover everything. This square is a broad tidal river of metal, cars pouring in and out in waves daily. The enormous slick of steel roofs laps against the houses, creates deep troughs, shimmers with the light ricocheting from rolled-up windows. One hundred, two hundred, three hundred cars: a gray beach of stones. Some places have been, by municipal decree, off-limits to them for some years now. But in many other historic town squares, like here in Piazza del Carmine, they are holding out. They seem to say, the cars: We're not leaving here, we have our emergency brakes on, we are locked with special keys and antitheft devices. We are staying here and holding out as long as we can.

Geometry | The square, the triangle, the octagon, and the circle: the architecture of Florence can be reduced to these four geometric shapes. Like no other city that I know, Florence is the place of geometry. Not in its city streets with their labyrinthine pattern but in its architecture, in the shape of its individual buildings. This geometric clarity is evident above all in the skyline of Florence, dominated by the hemisphere of the cathedral dome and the cubical body of Palazzo Vecchio. Pure, clear-cut forms, whose design is underlined by Brunelleschi's graphic signs or Arnolfo's precise masses.

The four original geometries stand out not only in

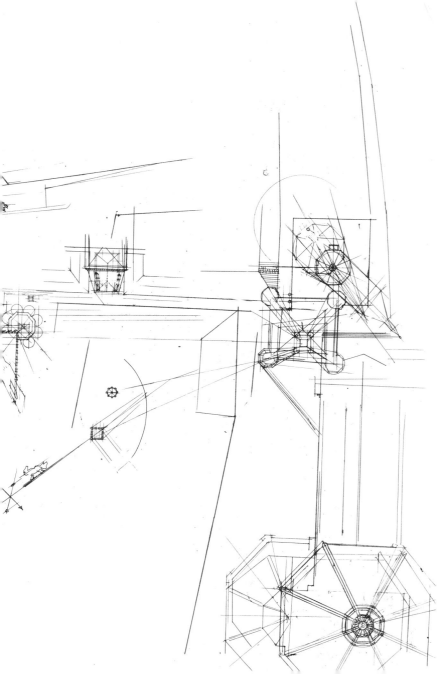

the volumes of the buildings but also in their ground plans and elevations:

The *square:* The primary shape of the Florentine palace courtyard is also the ground plan of the cloisters of the urban monasteries and the units of space covered by the cross vaults that make it up. Perfect cubes are Palazzo Strozzi and Orsanmichele, a pure parallelepiped is Giotto's bell tower.

The *triangle:* the image of the tympanums of Santa Croce, the spires of the bell towers (Santa Maria Novella, the Badia Fiorentina) or of the sharp-pointed bastions of the Forte di Belvedere.

The *octagon:* This is the shape that best identifies medieval Florence. Present in its first monument, the Baptistry, it reverberates on the scale of the landscape in the cathedral dome. Octagonal are the Gothic pillars of the churches, octagonal the sculpted plaques on Giotto's bell tower.

The *circle:* The epitome of the Renaissance ideal, this is the form of the central-plan buildings, the pioneering example of which was the church of Santa Maria degli Angeli, now an invisible relic. The circle appears on the vaults of the Pazzi Chapel, in the niches along the perimeter of Santo Spirito, in Brunelleschi's round windows. It is the golden sphere on top of the cathedral dome, the highest point in the whole city.

Every other important architectural monument is an elementary pairing of these geometric shapes. For example:

square/circle: the Old Sacristy in San Lorenzo, the church of Santo Spirito, and all the other architecture by Brunelleschi

circle/octagon: the dome and lantern of the cathedral, the interior dome of the Baptistry, the Medici Chapels at San Lorenzo

octagon/triangle: the ground plan and profile of the Badia Fiorentina bell tower

triangle/square: all the polychrome marble façades such as Santa Croce, San Miniato, Santa Maria Novella

Postwar Reconstruction | For people who do not know what happened in Florence during and after World War II, the area around the Ponte Vecchio must seem like some sort of architectural puzzle. Why is it, in such an ancient town center, that so many buildings do not look ancient? Why are so many façades overlooking the river a short distance from the Ponte Vecchio narrow curtain walls of glass? Where do those windows with incongruous roll blinds or concrete roof eaves come from?

In August 1944 the bridges of Florence were blown up by retreating German troops. Excepted from the devastation was the Ponte Vecchio. It seems that Hitler felt a special love for this bridge, so he decided to spare it, perhaps thinking about a future reconquest of the city. As an alternative, he ordered the destruction of the entire area around the bridge so that the rubble would slow down the advance of the Allied troops.

This was unquestionably the most tragic event in the thousand-year history of this city. It is a wound that disfigured—at the time, it seemed forever—the face of Florence, leaving the entire population in the most abject desperation.

When the war ended, the problem of the rebuilding of the area presented itself as an ethical and aesthetic issue. After endless debates on the character to give the new buildings, it was decided not to adopt a consistent, innovative project using the language of Modernist architecture but to assign the plots lined up along the old street routes to individual architects who would be held only to obeying strict urban planning rules. Many considered this to be just one more defeat of modern architecture in Italy, the classical missed chance in favor of the faceless pseudo-vernacular neutrality of the new buildings. As the years have passed, however, one has to admit that these new buildings, perhaps because of their modest architectural caliber, have so completely blended in with the historic urban fabric that the low-key contrast they offer has achieved a healthy, discreet balance.

These reflections of an architectural nature, however, leave another question unanswered: Why as one wanders about this part of the city is it impossible to find a plaque, a monument, no matter how small, an informative sign commemorating this tragic event? Is it only a case of absentmindedness on the part of the city administrators who have succeeded each other over the years? Was it thought that these memories would reawaken old pain? Or does this psychological-urbanistic "repression" spring from a desire not to have to rethink, and therefore detail, the various responsibilities for the destruction brought by the war?

Or, perhaps, has the idea prevailed that presenting a large part of the historic center as rebuilt *ex novo* in recent times would disappoint the many tourists who consider Florence to be a picturesque place, untouched and completely historic?

I Didn't Bring My Watercolors with Me |

I didn't bring my watercolors with me. If I had, now, leaning against this railing at Piazzale Michelangelo overlooking the fields toward the Forte di Belvedere, I would take out a sheet of paper, dip my brush in water, and mix my colors. First I would prepare a nice green,

as fresh as these April meadows right after a rain. With two or three brushstrokes I would draw an isosceles triangle with its top side horizontal to the skyline, one side slanting to the right where the city walls dip down into the city, and the third side slanting lower, interspersed with cypress trees. After mixing a darker green, almost black, I would make bold strokes from the bottom toward the top, lifting my brush as I go, to create cypresses with tops pointed like flames, some isolated and others joined together in a little woods. Next I would mix gray and blue, and spreading the color broadly, I would flood the entire upper half of the sheet with sky.

Then while this wash was drying, I would come back to the green of the fields, which would be dry by now, with quick touches of the brush in pink (the peach trees in bloom) and yellow ocher (the farmhouses). Taking a pencil, I would define some details: the branches of a distant pine tree, next to the outline of the Forte di Belvedere, the little windows of the houses on the meadows, the line of the city walls that make their way into the city, topped at intervals by square watchtowers. I would let the paper dry again. I would look at the landscape again and perhaps think that what I had done was only the interpretation of a given moment, of something that is always transformed with the changing seasons, the time of day, the intensity of the light, the weather, the point of view. That it was the vision of a landscape that is never the same, that changes over time along with the person who observes it, feels it, draws it, describes it—like me, in this precise moment, different from every other moment.

Toward San Miniato | Standing on the nineteenth-century boulevard (cars racing by, tires squealing on the pavement) and looking up, you can see, beyond the stone steps, the top of the façade of San Miniato. To reach the church, you have to climb this zigzagging staircase that, mutilating the original topography of the site, was built *ex novo* in the nineteenth century to give a more fitting, grander approach to the church. I wait for a break in the traffic and cross the street.

Now I am writing, stopping every so often as I climb the flights of steps as wide as marble waterfalls. At the first turn, the façade disappears from sight, but on the right, through the trees, the panorama of the city has appeared. After making the turn, I realize that there is a break in the steps to let a road pass through. This is useful for anyone who wants to approach the church more comfortably in a car. On the other side of the street, the stairs resume their course with a straight flight of at least a hundred steps. I climb at a slow, steady pace. It is a perfect staircase for a ritual: slowly ascending toward the marble façade, holding a bride's hand.

Halfway up the stairs I realize that I am in line with the façade, whose upper part I can only intuit. I observe the triangular tympanum, the glittering mosaic, the green stone arches, but not yet the portals—these are covered by the final flight of steps.

I face the last part, breathing more heavily now. When I reach the last landing I seat myself on a low precinct wall and write. I breathe. I look up, and I can see the façade, the whole thing.

The three portals are closed (it is late, evening by now) and there is not a living soul on the gravel in front of the church. But lower down, on the sides, are two areas covered with tombs. This is the most prestigious burial ground in the city, the cemetery of the Porte Sante al Monte alle Croci. I raise my eyes again to the front of the church. Two colors dominate: the white of the marble making up the background, the green of the stone creating countless designs. Only one small golden square breaks the spell—or rather, strengthens it. This is the central mosaic, in the Byzantine style, lit up by the rays of the setting sun, showing the Son of God with lifted hand protecting the city and its valley.

San Miniato, from outside, looks like a classical temple designed by a calligrapher from the Orient. A geometry of line constructed using a ruler, a triangle, and a compass. A precise, courageous line, and one that, if it were not so skillfully composed, would almost seem too much. A bold fantasy of overlapping and interlocking webs, then. This façade has influenced the history of Florentine art for centuries. It dictated its identity as "the city of line," so often compared with Venice, "the city of color." In the depth of a few centimeters a universe of possible readings is superimposed; a multitude of lines woven one on the other. It is as if the interior configuration of the church has been projected onto the exterior, on this one surface.

I get lost in looking more intensely at just one pilaster strip, then a panel of marble. I realize only now the countless details, the designs within the designs, the little inlaid mandala circles, the webs of lines that only someone coming from the East could repeat with such mastery, grafting them onto the perfect balance of Tuscan art.

Green Space | The relationship between Florence and "green space" (trees, parks, meadows, countryside) is quite ambiguous. The City of Flowers, whose cathedral is dedicated to Our Lady of the Flower, whose emblem is a flowering lily, owes this name to its particular geographical position and thus to the hills that enclose it on all sides in a tight embrace. The hills planted in olive trees, the manicured gardens, the rows of cypresses, the terraced fields of the countryside that ever since the founding of Florence come right up to the city gates and walls. It is still like this today. All you have to do is walk out of the Porta Romana or the Porta San Niccolò to see the contrast. On one side is the densely packed city, with houses piled up against each other along narrow streets. On the other, just a few meters beyond the walls, is the carefully laid out but unspoiled nature of the Tuscan countryside. All the ancient pictures of Florence clearly show this separation, this material contrast. The medieval town was defined by precise boundaries, even if inside the city walls there were ample areas designated for the vegetable gardens destined to ensure the population's survival in case of siege.

But Florence is also the city of large private parks, hidden behind the palaces and totally invisible from the street. First and foremost, the Boboli Gardens, the perfect synthesis of the art of the Italian garden from the fifteenth to the eighteenth century. The stony mass of Palazzo Pitti has acted as a bastion against the invasion of the "English garden" that was so popular in the nineteenth century. Included, too, are the immense

private parks like the Torrigiani gardens, which can barely be intuited beyond the walls along Viale Petrarca, or the equally immense Della Gherardesca gardens, which cannot be seen from anywhere except an airplane.

Walking through the historic center of Florence, one is not aware of these or any other urban green spaces. The impression is just the opposite: this is a city made of stone, arid as a quarry, waterless, with just a few scrawny trees. Only the nineteenth-century public squares and the broad boulevards, whose construction caused the complete demolition of the ancient walls, are there to present, with their abundance of trees, the vision of a healthy, and for those times "modern," city. It was the nineteenth century that gave us the great invention of the Parco delle Cascine, which today has lost much of its former prestige. It is not the popular, elegant promenade it was in its time, the symbol of the union between nature, recreation, and culture. It is for the most part a group of functions separate from each other (the racetrack, the meadow, the university, the pool, the nightclub) and as a further social magnet it is reduced to a place for jogging and the site of the open-air market on Tuesdays.

Finding other green space is not easy: the boundless periphery is arid, full of concrete, made up only of walls and pavement. Something that might resemble a real park may appear in the new neighborhood in Novoli, in the area formerly occupied by the Fiat plant; or, farther away, on the Castello plain. But for now, all we can do is appreciate what was already there since the fourteenth century—the countryside that descends intact all the way into the city. Fortunately, but not without problems, a great local architect, Edoardo Detti, who was assigned the task of drawing up a town-planning scheme in the 1960s, fought to keep real-estate speculation from taking over the hills of Fiesole, Settignano, Bellosguardo, and Arcetri in a sort of siege from within. The urban regulations forbade anyone, without exceptions, to touch those hills. Some accused Detti of not keeping up with the times, but today we all thank him for maintaining one of the most beautiful, healthy, and harmonious examples of the relationship between architecture and landscape.

A Certain Slant of Light | There is a specific time when one should stop to admire the façade of Palazzo Vecchio. This is the moment when the sun's rays strike it from the side, highlighting to the utmost the pattern of its stone blocks. In those few brief moments, the façade, accentuated by the shadows cast by its rough surface, takes on a dazzling three-dimensionality. That

hour is precisely 12:30 P.M. every day during the winter, and an hour later, at 1:30, when daylight savings time is in effect. This occurs for two reasons. The façade faces west, so at noon the rays of the sun, which at that moment is due south, rake across its surface from the side. This event takes place every single noncloudy day at the same time regardless of season. In the summer the sun is higher on the horizon, and in the winter lower. One could think that in the winter the buildings standing around the edge of Piazza della Signoria would hide the sun's rays. But this does not happen, for—and this is the second reason—the Uffizi buildings, with their north-south orientation, seem to have been designed precisely in order to let these rays through at noon. Conceived on a plan like an elongated U with its open side facing Palazzo Vecchio, the Uffizi buildings act like a funnel for the sun's rays that at exactly 12:30 every day (or at 1:30 during daylight savings time) illuminate the south side of every single stone on the façade.

In other cases, too, we could decide the best time of day to admire a certain piece of architecture. We could establish a refined, special hour, as though suggested by a skillful exhibition curator who knows exactly the best light to focus on the side of a building, spire, a dome, a porch or statue. We will call this "a guide to the hours of the day." I can already imagine a graphic symbol associated with each monument: a little sun with next to it the best time of day to enjoy the sight.

The Fountains | Every city has its own particular relationship with water. Seas, rivers, lakes are the natural elements that often define the identity of a place. Some cities evidence another special symbiosis in the artificial organization of water in canals, ditches, artificial lakes, and, finally, fountains. In Florence, "water" first and foremost means the waters of the Arno. This is a river capable of doing anything: of drying up almost completely in the summer, or of swelling mightily and overflowing its banks, as it has done more than once in recent centuries.

Florence is not a city of fountains, but their presence can be perceived.

There is a major one right in the heart of the city. It was dedicated to Neptune, the sea god, to celebrate the Medici principality's access to the Tyrrhenian Sea, gained by the conquest of Leghorn. It is a quite beautiful fountain, a masterpiece of figures in marble and bronze. Positioned at the corner of Palazzo Vecchio, it accentuates the angular form of Piazza della Signoria.

In Piazza Santissima Annunziata there are two foun-

tains, exactly the same; virtuoso examples of bronze work. With a brilliant stroke of insight, the Baroque sculptor who made them created twin fountains set at a distance from each other, but by mirroring the bilateral symmetry of the whole square, they interpret perfectly the spectacular nature of the site. In a stroke of brilliance, each individual fountain has been divided into two symmetrical parts, the left half a mirror image of the right: a game of mirrors, starting from the details of the bronze and going on to the entire concept of the urban void.

The other type of fountain is the kind comprising an octagonal basin with a central spout and a faucet for drinking water. In Piazza Santo Spirito, such a fountain is placed precisely in the center of the space; in Piazza Santa Croce it is located on the central axis, but moved to the side opposite from the church. These were the fountains where people went to fill their jars and jugs until a century ago. Then there are smaller fountains that are often exquisite sculptural exercises in symbiosis with the water. Two come to mind: the fountain of the Porcellino, or wild boar, at the open-air market of the Mercato Nuovo, an imaginative reworking in bronze of a Roman sculpture now in the Uffizi Gallery; and the bizarre Triton embracing a thick marble shell in the midst of a curly sea. It is on the acute angle formed by the intersection of Via Maggio with Via dello Sprone.

This is more or less all the public water in Florence. And yet there is hidden water too: the water that splashes inside the grottoes at the back of private gardens and with its gurgling feeds the lichen clinging to stalactites made of plaster or stone. Or it is the water at the bottom of wells in the middle of cloisters, or the small, sacred store of water in the holy water fonts or the baptisteries.

In Florence, there is a large garden where water plays a leading role. In the Boboli Gardens, lined up with Palazzo Pitti, there is a big green amphitheater which has an immense ancient Roman granite basin in the middle of it. The basin, mounted on a pedestal, is a pure archeological object, empty and waterless. A bit lower down, at the end of a long avenue sloping downhill, is the most extensive fountain in the city, an entire round plaza devoted once again to Neptune, nymphs, and Tritons. The empty basin on the one hand, the flooded plaza on the other, two metaphoric poles of the water in Florence: an arid, dry, stony city, and a flowering city, lapped by the water of the river and, very often, even flooded by it.

At Night, in the Summer | It is a summer's night, the window is open, and I lie stretched out, a bit sweaty, on the sheets. Only after many breaths do I hear a car pass.

I know that beyond the roofs is the huge red dome, incandescent; the palace and the tower, illuminated; the façade of Santa Croce, her piazza bathed in soft light, dim alleyways, dark passages, black corners, where someone is leaning while kissing or talking or trying some substance that will or will not bring happiness. Between that obscure point and this bed, this writing hand, there is a common thread: this moment in the city.

ILLUSTRATIONS

Some years ago, during a hot, silent, deserted August, I purposely left my usual watercolors sketchbook at home and decided to wander around Florence equipped with only a notebook and pen. I wanted to verify the power of the word, as opposed to drawing, to describe the city. The result of that initial experiment is this little book.

The fact is that my interest as an architect has always been focused on representing the city by means of drawing, either from life or from memory. Like thin, flexible mirrors, the pages of this book reflect writings and drawings back and forth to each other, letting a mutual echo expand between them.

Readers will find evident convergences or inexplicable contradictions between these two *modi operandi:* I leave the judgment up to them. As far as I am concerned, the question is still open: Which of the two descriptions of the city is more pleasing, closer to reality, more capable of stimulating the imagination, the drawn or the written? To tell the truth, I would like not to have to choose, but to go on exploring, contemporaneously, both of these boundless territories.

Map of Florence

The station

The river

Loggia del Mercato Nuovo

The green riverbank

Piazza del Carmine

Via Santo Spirito

Piazza Santo Spirito

Arcetri

Enter

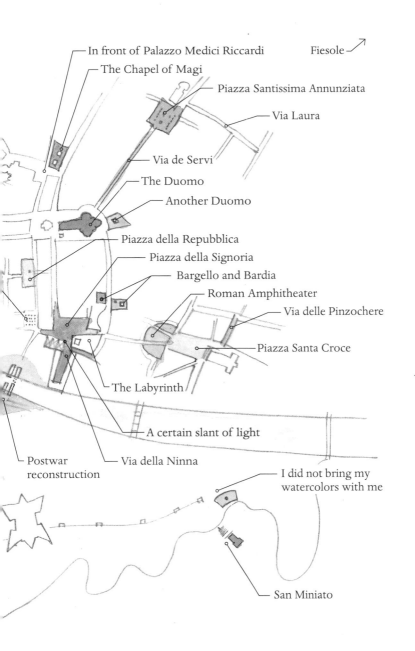

In front of Palazzo Medici Riccardi

Fiesole

The Chapel of Magi

Piazza Santissima Annunziata

Via Laura

Via de Servi

The Duomo

Another Duomo

Piazza della Repubblica

Piazza della Signoria

Bargello and Bardia

Roman Amphitheater

Via delle Pinzochere

Piazza Santa Croce

The Labyrinth

A certain slant of light

Postwar reconstruction

Via della Ninna

I did not bring my watercolors with me

San Miniato

ACKNOWLEDGMENTS

A special thanks to Patricia Sachs, James Saywell, and Susan Scott for translating parts of the manuscript from the Italian; to Boyd Zenner for her encouragement and crucial professional support; and to Kitty, to whom I dedicate this book.